DAVID E. JOHNSTON MA

ROMAN VILLAS

Fourth edition

SHIRE ARCHAEOLOGY

Cover illustration
A model of the villa at Sparsholt, Hampshire.
(David E. Johnston)

British Library Cataloguing in Publication Data
Johnston, David E.
Roman Villas. – 4Rev.ed. – (Shire Archaeology Series; No. 11)
I. Title. II. Series.
936.204
ISBN 0-7478-0238-6

Published in 1994 by
SHIRE PUBLICATIONS LTD
Cromwell House, Church Street, Princes Risborough,
Buckinghamshire HP27 9AJ, UK.

Series Editor: James Dyer

ISBN 0 7478 0238 6

First edition 1979; second edition 1983; third edition 1988,
fourth edition 1994.

Printed in Great Britain by
CIT Printing Services, Press Buildings,
Merlins Bridge, Haverfordwest, Dyfed SA61 1XF.

Contents

4

List of illustrations

Preface

This book has been written for the general reader, as an introduction to an exciting and developing part of the story of Roman Britain. For over a century interest in villas remained fixed on the bricks-and-mortar aspects, and it is only recently — as the dates of the books listed on page 25 confirm — that both our thinking and improved techniques of gathering the evidence have brought about a much fuller understanding of what the villas really were. In 1969 the first book devoted entirely to the subject concluded with a chapter on 'The Future of Villa Studies'; some years later this present book, which is little more than an interim summary, endeavours to show how far our understanding has advanced. The balance of topics reflects the balance of current thinking, as well as admitting the major uncertainties that still exist; while the sheer quantity of sites to choose from has made the task of selection quite painful. But the reader whose interest is aroused and whose questions remain unanswered is invited to pursue the subject through the books recommended for the purpose.

In preparing the text and illustrations I have drawn heavily on the published and unpublished work of others, in many cases redrawing and reinterpreting; I am deeply grateful to those numerous friends and colleagues who have allowed me to do so and discussed their work with me. I have also to thank the following institutions and individuals for providing photographic illustrations: the Department of the Environment (plates 1, 18); Professor J. K. St Joseph and the Cambridge University Committee for Aerial Photography (plates 3, 4, 10); the Ashmolean Museum, Oxford (plate 6); the University of Southampton (plate 12); Mr W. G. Putnam and the Dorset Institute for Higher Education (plate 13); Professor K. Branigan (plate 16); Mr J. Brown (plate 17); Mr J. Dettmar (plate 15); Mr M. J. Locke (plate 13); Mr C. de la Nougerede (plate 9); Mr D. Tomalin (plate 8), Colonel P. Walters (plates 5, 11) and the Roman Research Trust, Littlecote (plate 7). The British Museum kindly gave permission to reproduce both drawings in fig. 18.

1
What is a villa?

Attempts to define a villa usually seem to end in vagueness or — even more confusingly — in utter disagreement among scholars. To a Roman the answer would have been simple: a villa is a farm. To the archaeologist, who has to be careful with his technical terms, there are two quite distinct sides to the picture. On one side is the traditional idea of the villa as the 'country house' of a Romanised Briton; and we must be quite clear at the outset that we are thinking not of Romans from Rome (of whom there were few in Britain outside the army) but of the inhabitants of a Roman province, who were 'Romans' in a more general sense. To many of these people the new regime brought opportunities for wealth and expensive tastes, and these are reflected in the mosaics, wall paintings, dining rooms and sumptuous baths that we all associate with the villas. Such men were often the old aristocracy of pre-Roman Britain serving as councillors and magistrates in the cities. The new towns and cities had introduced a way of life that was impossible in pre-Roman Britain, and so we can think of the villas as taking the luxuries of town life into the countryside. The other side of the picture is more mundane, but equally absorbing. It is of the villa as a farm, a food-producing machine. In archaeological terms we have to identify an estate, with forests, meadows and cultivated fields; we have to excavate grouped or scattered buildings that can range from cowsheds to corn-driers, from watermills to wine cellars. The estate produced, and to a large degree also processed, not only food but other animal products (leather, tallow, wool, etc) and the timber that was used in far greater quantities than today. So we occasionally find evidence for tanning and fulling, and a few villas were truly 'industrial', being attached to potteries and tile-kilns. Hunting, fowling and fishing were more than mere recreation; they were the proper exploitation of all the natural resources of a varied estate.

Not all villas were run for private profit, however. The small farmer could have been a tenant or bailiff of a landowner who might live as far away as North Africa, with property in many provinces, or a tenant, perhaps of the state — that is, of the Emperor. Clues to state ownership have been, for instance, a

Keep up to date on the latest books from Shire.

Send for regular free catalogues by completing this card.

Name ....

Address ....

....

....

.... Postcode ....

Let us know your special interests.

☐ Antiques/collecting ☐ Fashion/needlecrafts
☐ Archaeology ☐ Garden history
☐ Architecture ☐ Industrial history
☐ Canals and ships ☐ Military history
☐ Egyptology ☐ Natural history
☐ Ethnography ☐ Railways
☐ Farming bygones ☐ Road Transport

SI 93

Shire Publications Ltd,
Cromwell House,
Church Street,
Princes Risborough,
Buckinghamshire
HP27 9AJ.

lead seal or an inscription. Moreover, the owner-occupier had to part with much, even most, of his produce in tax, which was collected in kind. At Hambleden, Buckinghamshire, for example, there was huge capacity for 'drying' the corn (see fig. 19), but no granaries for storing it; and the discovery of no less than seventy *stili* (bronze pens) points to bureaucratic checking of the produce, which was presumably collected and moved elsewhere — much of it doubtless to the military garrisons of north Britain. In times of civil war the estates of those on the losing side were confiscated by the state; in peacetime, though this is hard to establish, they were bought, sold or amalgamated. In the troubled times elsewhere of the third century AD there are signs that continental entrepreneurs were investing in property in Britain. By the end of the period inflation was running high, and the financial burdens of civic office that landowning entailed were becoming insupportable. Only the largest estates could survive, with small farmers and peasants locked in a circle of debt and bondage that amounted almost to serfdom. The father's occupation was now legally binding on the son, and those who abandoned their work or property could be rounded up like slaves. This is the social background to some, at least, of the villas in this book.

We may be wrong to think of a single owner in every case. A recent theory, which has yet to win general acceptance, suggests two, three or more families to a villa. This certainly makes sense at Newton St Loe, Avon (fig. 1), with two self-sufficient houses next to each other; at Bignor, Sussex, with up to four units (fig. 4); or at Chedworth, Gloucestershire, where a duplicate suite of living and dining rooms, kitchen and baths was provided in the north wing. But we cannot identify or describe a single individual owner. A certain Faustinus owned a villa in Norfolk that we have yet to find; in plate 1 we may be looking at a portrait of an owner or his wife; and we would like to put life back into the young couple buried in the family mausoleum in the grounds of the Lullingstone villa (plate 18). Here we can at least trace the religious beliefs of successive owners (fig. 5). In the second century part of the house was a shrine to three water goddesses (seen painted in a niche), while a later family converted the rooms above to a Christian house-church. Many villa owners were Christian — one, at Hinton St Mary, Dorset, boldly commissioning a mosaic floor showing the head of Christ and scenes of paradise (now in the British Museum). Others, however, were understandably ambiguous in their professions of faith. How far their employees followed suit we cannot say; who, for instance, carved the little Christian sign, possibly on the fountain, or water shrine, at Chedworth? Ambiguity and secrecy, of course, were characteristic of the pagan 'mystery' religions, and it is suggested that the detached dining and reception complex of the newly excavated villa at Littlecote, Berkshire, was the meeting place of such a cult; certainly, there is much uncertainty over the religious meaning of the mosaics, and an alternative view sees the building (which was unheated) merely as a summer dining-room. There are similarly cryptic mosaics in the villa at Brading, Isle of Wight (fig. 3).

It must always be remembered that agriculture was not the only basic activity of a villa. The 'industrial' villas (Castor, Cambridgeshire, and Ashtead, Surrey, for example) could each have been the residence of the proprietor of an industrial concern. The villa at Coombe Down, Wiltshire, was — according to an inscription — the *principia* or 'headquarters' of something official, presumably a state-run estate or quarries producing stone for public buildings. The isolated tower-block at Stonea, Cambridgeshire, was certainly the 'head office' of an imperial estate. We shall also see below that the Gadebridge Park villa became a specialised 'health farm' or private spa. Some 'villas', moreover, seem to have been merely part of a much larger community or settlement. It is now thought that the walled complex at Gatcombe, Somerset, is not a small town but rather a large villa of a type familiar on the continent (where, for example, a certain Cruptorix described his long-house and settlement as a *villa*). Peculiarities in the archaeological record of other British villas suggest that the term should in future embrace large rural communities of this kind. Nevertheless, at this stage in our thinking we cannot truly say that we understand the real nature of some of our larger establishments.

We are on firmer ground when we return finally to the economic significance of the villa. From the earliest years of the occupation it was a functional response to new, heavy demands on the peasant farmer — the growing markets in the new towns, the requisitions for the army of occupation, and above all the demands of the tax-collector. Although life in the fields and villages may have looked much the same as it had for centuries, everyone felt the pressures of central government. This, then, is how the villas came into being, not only in Britain but in most of the western Empire: the adaptation of a Celtic way of life to the requirements of the classical world.

2
The simple house

The Roman occupation lasted nearly four hundred years — as long as from the time of Queen Elizabeth I to the present day — and the changes over that period were equally profound. So we must expect the major villas, like any country house, to have evolved often unrecognisably from their simple beginnings. Some later examples emerged fully fledged from the drawing board, while a few remained cottages, without elaboration; generally, however, we find a simple 'cottage-house' embedded in something more complex.

Plate 3 shows a three-roomed cottage built on the vanished remains of an iron age ditched settlement that had been disused, perhaps, for a century or more. Even if the general choice of site was deliberate, its precise position, over the softer filling of the lost ditches, must be accidental. Earlier ditches can be seen running under the house in plate 5. In plate 4 the ghost of an earlier, one-roomed house on a different alignment can be seen beneath the nearer end; and a further room has apparently been added at the other. Beyond it, a circular stone building is probably Roman, but copying the shape of the typical pre-Roman native hut. The other two face away from the farmyard, whose wall can be traced. Although unexcavated, this site shows a simple evolution and a differentiation of function that we cannot yet explain.

We have some dates for our next example, Lockleys, near Welwyn. Casual pre-Roman occupation is shown by a circular hut and other features. The first Roman house, of timber, was built between AD 50 and 120 and subsequently removed, leaving only a row of post-holes. The first stone-built house is a late example of a strip-house (about AD 300) that soon had a pair of wings added, with a corridor or verandah in front, to look like fig. 7. The slope of the ground allowed the rarity of an upper floor at the nearer end. The further modifications followed a fire in about AD 340.

The resultant 'winged corridor plan' is clearly seen at Park Street, St Albans (fig. 8), where a strip-house was similarly incorporated, in the middle of the second century AD. These modifications are very significant; the rectangular stone strip-houses show the impact of Rome on a Celtic land where the circular hut was the normal house form. Subsequently the widespread adoption of the wings and corridor, or pillared verandah (as in the example on our cover), represents an architectural cliché universal throughout the Empire — the pillared, classical facade. But there is more to it than this; in the strip-house, the rooms were probably interconnected, of equal importance and with little privacy. The corridor allowed a hierarchy of rooms, the separation of heads of the family and other members of the household, and a range of different uses for the rooms. Structurally, too, the changes were important; the roof structure was complicated and less light reached the main rooms. Windows therefore were restricted to the open side, with either clerestory lights or dormers above the verandah. Consequently the main walls and the ceilings (if any) had to be taller, making the rooms more elegant and airy. When a further range of rooms was provided at the back, as in the main house at Brading, Isle of Wight (fig. 3), the problems of lighting must have been acute. The roofs sometimes carried ventilators and chimney-pots. Fireplaces with hoods, to burn charcoal or coal, were occasionally fitted, as at Newport, Isle of Wight (fig. 16). Frequently these and the hypocausts vented under the eaves, as can be seen in the nearer wing of plate 8.

On the whole the functions of individual rooms elude us, though we can sometimes guess in very simple cases, such as fig. 6. Here we can imagine a quiet, private end (the 'study' was heated by a brazier), a fine central reception and dining-room with mosaic (accessible, admittedly, to livestock from the farmyard outside) and a warm but noisy end, with kitchen, servants' room (a 'squalid, smoky den' according to the excavator) and a room warmed by the gentle, steady heat of a channelled (not pillared) hypocaust. Bedrooms are hard to identify, though one room at Lullingstone had two depressions in the floor, containing coins, each perhaps under the head of a mattress or narrow bed. Generally, however, the Roman couch (a 'day-bed', like a chaise longue) was used for sleeping, and in a villa any living-room could serve as a bedroom. Kitchens were disappointingly uncomplicated, the principal feature being a hearth or masonry block upon which a charcoal fire was lit under a gridiron so that pots could be simmered and meat grilled. Bathrooms were usually either detached (because of the fire risk) or placed at one end of the range (e.g. fig. 16). Lavatories are found in towns rather than in villas (perhaps because of the proximity of suitable tree cover), and domestic rubbish was disposed of in pits or out of the window (as at Sparsholt, where a heap accumulated among the nettles in an angle of the outside walls where nobody ever went). Excavators often encounter burials of newborn infants, either as a dedication (fig. 6) or the surreptitious evidence of unofficial births on the villa. There were ninety-seven at Hambleden, where the farmyard 'was positively littered with babies'. Finally, indoor shrines must have existed, but they or their contents are seldom recognised.

3
The complex villa

Frocester Court, Gloucestershire (fig. 10), has a compact main house (which also evolved from a strip-house) and a fine display of ditched enclosures around a walled courtyard. There are two gardens (a feature rarely identified in Roman Britain); that behind the house had soil suitable for vegetables, while in front were formal flowerbeds flanking the gravel drive with its turning area (fig. 13). These were omitted over an earlier cemetery that was left turfed, while a narrow hedge apparently screened an external stokehole from the view of visitors. Elsewhere, as at Chedworth (fig. 11) and Latimer, Buckinghamshire (fig. 12), we can make only an intelligent guess at the layout of flowerbeds, hedges, trees and kitchen gardens. The Ditchley villa (plate 6) was clearly approached by a drive between paddocks or orchards.

The courtyard wall at this villa enclosed a farmyard with a well (the dark spot) and circular threshing-floor. Such a coherent layout usually evolved over a period, as in fig. 23, where lack of privacy in the aisled building is thought to have driven the owner to build his new house nearby, forming the beginning of a symmetrical ensemble. The more complex sequence at Gade-bridge Park included the removal of the main yard from one side of the house to the other (fig. 24). By now (early fourth century) the main attractions were the new heated rooms (under the tower-like wings of fig. 14), the rebuilt bath suite and the large swimming pool (an unusual feature). As the waters may have been curative, the villa could have functioned less as a farm than as a 'health farm' or private spa. The final phases of these two villas are discussed in chapter 7. The apparent disintegration of a unified house plan is seen in the final phase at Park Street (fig. 8), while a masterpiece of conversion is seen at Rapsley, Ewhurst, Surrey, in the left-hand building of plate 9. The architect has defied boggy and uneven ground to transform a compact orthodox bath-house by stages into a convincing winged corridor dwelling-house.

Villas like Chedworth with a double courtyard, doubtless a farmyard and a private garden, display a deceptive unity. There is now little sign of the three original buildings sharing a common bath suite and water shrine; nor of the independent family unit apparently provided at the end of the north wing. The great establishment at Brading, Isle of Wight (fig. 3), was also probably in two parts, the better known half consisting of a winged corridor house (now attractively displayed to visitors) flanked tidily by aisled buildings with others perhaps beyond. In the great villas of Gaul the main house frequently looked out on two rows of outbuildings (often not parallel but diverging to enhance the effect of distance); this continental style may be reflected in plate 10, an unexcavated site where the main house and its neighbour (at the top of the photograph) look out on at least two carefully placed outbuildings. The intermediate phase at Bignor, West Sussex (fig. 4), was of this tapering, Gaulish plan. In its final form this unity has been abandoned; the private parts are completely secluded, although house and farmyard (4½ acres, 1.8 hectares, in all) are enclosed by a single unifying wall. Visitors to this pleasant site can trace the earlier phases marked in coloured concrete. The likely function of the farm buildings is discussed in chapter 6. Rockbourne, Hampshire (fig. 2), is another large complex probably enclosing a farmyard and private garden, whose full plan is still not known. At these three sites visitors can see only a part of the excavated remains and must use their imagination to visualise the grandeur of the whole.

North Leigh, Oxfordshire, has two wings open to view, and the other two can be easily traced on the ground, and air photographs have shown that an equally large complex of farm buildings, enclosed by a wall and divided by a gravel road, still exists beneath adjoining farm land.

The most unified and magnificent plan was that of Woodchester, Gloucestershire, though here, too, the splendid mansion with it columned reception room and Orpheus mosaic was merely the nucleus of a more extensive establishment. This palatial layout is more Mediterranean than British in conception and is remarkable in this distant northern province. The same can be said of Fishbourne, West Sussex, which was truly a palace and strictly is outside the scope of this book. Today visitors can still marvel at the mosaics, courtyards and formal gardens so skilfully recreated. But looking at the excellent model in the museum one can easily forget two important points: first, that like Woodchester this was merely a nucleus of an estate that comprised private, park-like grounds sweeping southwards to the seashore and a small private harbour, and that around it, to the north, apparently spread a small community of servants' quarters, workshops and farm buildings that have yet to be fully traced. Second, this 10 acre (4

hectare) building ceased to be a palace as early as about AD 100
and was split up into separate units. Further modifications were
abruptly terminated by a disastrous fire at the end of the third
century, but the process if continued would have rendered
Fishbourne virtually indistinguishable from any of the wealthier
villas of Britain. A link with the rest is an aisled building in the
north-east corner.

4
Architecture and interior decoration

From the earliest days of the occupation the design and
construction of British villas was as high as anywhere in the
Empire. In particular, the bath suite displays a design as
advanced as its way of life was alien to Britain. For the baths were
more than a source of cleanliness: they were a warm, noisy and
unhurried place of recreation and their decoration was often very
lavish. At Chedworth, as in a few other villas, the bather was
even offered a choice of two procedures — the 'Spartan' and the
ordinary. The first entailed dry heat and high temperatures, on
the sauna principle; the second, akin to the Turkish bath, used
damp heat and plunge baths. The basic sequence is well
exemplified in the small house (which can be visited today) at
Newport, Isle of Wight (fig. 16). From the unheated changing
room *(apodyterium)* the bather passed through a warm room
(tepidarium) — or two in this case — next to the *caldarium* which
contained a hot bath. The hot, steamy atmosphere opened the
pores of the skin and induced sweating; the dirt was removed not
with soap but with oil and a curved *strigil,* or scraper. Massage
could be part of the process, which continued with a leisurely
return through the warm room to the *frigidarium,* to end with a
sharp cold plunge and a rub down with a towel. In public baths
the latrine is found here, flushed by the same water supply (plate
14). Architecturally the baths could be the showpiece of the villa
(at Lufton, for instance, fig. 17), while the elaborate example at
Stroud (fig. 9) was undoubtedly an amenity for a very large
estate.

Complex bath suites were architecturally very sophisticated.
The diagram in fig. 16 is based on the simple specimen shown on
the cover, and it illustrates the ingenuity with which the warmth
was conserved and used. The hot air and gases passed under the
hypocaust floor and up a jacket of box-flues concealed in the
walls. Sometimes these vented under the eaves, but sometimes
they led to hollow brick ribs. These distinctive voussoir-shaped
flues have often gone unrecognised by excavators; they were used
at Bignor, and sharp eyes can detect them in the modern paving
at the entrance, while a specimen has recently been placed in the
museum. Tufa is a porous limestone like breeze-block, ideal for

an insulated vault. The insulation was completed by narrow lancet windows, glazed with pale green glass. The hot bath emptied into a drain, made of logs joined by iron collars, and the bald concrete vaults were discovered (after the model on the cover was made) to have been roofed with tiles. There were two kinds of hypocaust: the pillared variety could be heated more rapidly as required, while the masonry masses of the chanelled kind acted like block-storage heaters and were more suitable for living rooms.

Roofs were of thatch, tiles or stone slates, occasionally in combination (as on the cover), crested with semicircular ridge-tiles and finished with terracotta or stone finials (plate 13). Most museums can demonstrate the characteristic combination of curved *imbrex* and flat *tegula* giving an effect like large pantiles.

Walls were generally timber-framed on low sill-walls, and the timbering was often rendered — though the scratched sketch of a villa from Hucclecote, now in the British Museum (fig. 18), seems to show exposed timbers. Windows were rarely glazed, probably because of the expense, the panes being held in place by cross-shaped iron devices where the window bars crossed. Wooden shutters must have been normal. Interior walls were regularly painted, and good modern excavation is constantly recovering excellent, if fragmentary, murals. Examples can be seen at Bignor and Lullingstone, while Winchester Museum has on display some outstanding material. Doors were either hinged or made with stout vertical pins turning in metal bushes in the lintel and threshold. Locks and keys can be found in most museums.

Wall mosaics were rare, but most villas could boast one or more fine mosaic floors, and wherever possible these are now displayed on the site. Cheaper floors were of coarse red *tesserae*, perhaps with carpets, or of concrete, pink plaster, even bare earth. A few houses had painted ceilings.

Of furniture we know disappointingly little; the elegant rooms recreated in the museums of Cirencester and London show what could have been found in any well appointed villa, with cupboards, sideboards and occasional tables set against the walls. The classical dining room or *triclinium*, with diners reclining on couches arranged in threes, sometimes appears in Britain in the apsed rooms that can be seen, for instance, at Bignor and Lullingstone. We must accept, however, that in the north-western provinces most people ate at tables with chairs or couches in square dining rooms.

Finally, the existence of upper floors is much debated. Walls of exceptional thickness and narrow rooms that might have contained stairs are thought to be clues. At Chalk the wooden stairs survived, with cupboard space below. A staircase is suggested on fig. 10.

It is now generally assumed that the more ambitious villas (e.g. plate 7) followed Roman practice elsewhere and had at least two storeys.

5
Aisled barns and other buildings

It will be clear by now that the villa was seldom a single building, however luxurious. The other buildings of the complex reflect — insofar as we can ever be sure of their uses — the varied activities of the farm. The need for accommodation for resident labourers leads us to a fairly common multi-purpose building, the *aisled building* (sometimes called basilican, as it has a nave and two aisles). Many villas had one of these; a few had two. In them were probably stored equipment and produce (but never, it seems, animals). Certainly they housed large numbers of people and gave cover for indoor activities such as corn drying and metal working. At Sparsholt a single cooking range against one wall was surrounded by ashes and trampled food debris — clearly a communal kitchen and focal point on cold winter evenings. The conjectural reconstruction of a typical example in fig. 15 shows a cart-sized entrance at one side (or sometimes at the end), a timber-framed construction on low sleeper-walls and stone pillar-bases, and a simple roof carried down to the walls in a single sweep. Opinions vary on this last point, and the model on the cover shows an alternative solution to the problem of lighting and ventilation (still a single-storey affair, perhaps with a hayloft above). The type is best regarded as a British invention, though closely similar buildings occasionally occur on the continent.

Privacy was at a premium and many aisled buildings show signs of temporary partitions making improvised compartments or rooms (the dotted lines on fig. 15). These would 'fossilise' and become more permanent, so that in some evolved examples only the proportions and a few surviving pillar-bases reveal the original layout. Occasionally, as at Brading, the baths for the whole community were incorporated. Often, as at North Warnborough, this remained the principal building, the only farmhouse, and underwent extensive modifications — in this case a kind of modernisation with twin towers, or wings, to improve the facade. Sparsholt is unique in having two, apparently of similar plan, superimposed (fig. 15 and plate 11). Here the owner eventually moved out and constructed his new bungalow nearby (see cover); but not before he had created three private rooms for himself and his family, one with a tessellated floor, another with a mosaic. Perhaps he left these to his farm manager. A pair of heavily modified aisled buildings can be detected on the plan of Brading (fig. 3).

The barn or granary was another necessary building sometimes detached (as in the corner of the Ditchley villa, to the right of the entrance), but often incorporated in the range of outbuildings. The raised floor is sometimes indicated by an offset in the walls (Stroud, fig. 9) or by parallel supporting walls (North Warnborough), and frequently by buttresses (the north-east block at Woodchester). The dimensions sometimes enable a reasoned guess to be made at other buildings; three stalls, for instance, in the long barn at Stroud could have held three teams of oxen while twelve plough teams could have been accommodated in a long building in the yard at Bignor. An earlier long building (later demolished) at Bignor (fig. 4) is interpreted as a cattle-shed, and the small granary at Stroud has suggested the grain-fattening of pigs in the adjoining building.

All this is guesswork, but there is no doubt about the huge barn just visible in the corner of the view of Lullingstone (plate 18). Notice also the circular mill or threshing-floor in the yard at Ditchley (plate 6). A rare find at Fullerton, Hampshire, was evidence for a watermill, though unhappily only the mill leat and the debris of the mill itself survived.

Finally, an isolated outbuilding of a lost villa at Chalk, near Gravesend, excavated by the writer, excited some speculation. This was an oblong one-roomed house, with timber-framed walls, painted wall plaster and a tiled roof. Standing near the entrance to the complex, it might have belonged to the bailiff. Below it was a cellar, entered by wooden steps, lit by lamps in niches and with a ramp for rolling down barrels. It was a wine cellar of a well known pattern. Later this too received painted wall plaster and became a dwelling. In its final phase, however, this basement is thought to have been an *ergastulum,* or slave prison. Large fetters were found, and infant burials in the floor. One of its last occupants had sat near the doorway making pins from antler and jet. Here we found his pewter dish and spoon, his knife and a whetstone. A discarded boot (or at least its studs) completed the untidy picture. Whether this villa employed slaves we shall never know for certain; but one pottery sherd strengthens the suggestion (plate 12), as it was inscribed in Greek characters *FELICI (TER)* — 'To Felix' or perhaps 'Good luck'. A Greek clerk would certainly have been an asset on any Romano-British villa.

6
The villa estate

The Frocester Court villa (fig. 10) illustrates the diversity of a typical estate, focused on the 'office' with its strong-box, central hearth and coin scatter. The living rooms were in the south-east corner (probably on two floors), with the 'corn room' (corn-drier and quern) later converted into a kitchen. About AD 360 the baths were added in place of the open-fronted 'wool shed' in which quantities of fuller's earth were found, for fulling and felting. Close to the villa was a dipping pool, and a sheep-bell was among the finds. The western paddock could have been useful for animals awaiting shoeing at the forge or milking. Horse bones, especially those of young animals, were comparatively common and oats were certainly grown, so commercial horse-breeding is a possibility. Pannage for pigs would have been provided by forests on the estate, and bones of chicken, duck and goose have also been found.

The crops — barley, three varieties of wheat and oats — were described by a specialist as 'well-grown, clean, healthy crops which had been harvested and stored under ideal conditions'. Other Romano-British farmers — to judge from recent analyses — were more tolerant of weeds, even perhaps encouraging a deliberate mixture. Cereals were not only for human consumption but also for grain-fattening of pigs for bacon, while other crops such as rape, vetch and turnip, as well as hay, were winter-feed for cattle. Over-wintering cattle was more successful in Roman times than ever before, with the additional assistance of cowsheds, wells (virtually a Roman introduction) and straw (as the new low-cutting scythe superseded the prehistoric practice of cutting only the ears). Crop rotation was recommended by Roman text-books, as was the sowing of both spring and winter wheat, and the importance of manure is deduced from the use of animal pens and the distribution of household debris in fields far from the house. Viticulture, although officially permitted, was not widespread. An important development, which matches the pre-Roman change from storing grain in pits to granaries, is the construction of 'corn-driers' (fig. 19); parching facilitates threshing and milling and prevents germination in store. However, recent experiments have suggested that they are inefficient at drying corn, although they are ideal for malting.

The range of tools used is illustrated in fig. 20, and most are types familiar to us today. The quern is a hand-mill (properly known as an 'oscillatory' rather than a 'rotary' quern as the movement was roughly a quarter-turn). This was a pre-Roman invention, for domestic use, while the large villa could afford a full-size animal-driven mill and one Hampshire estate had a watermill. Spades were of wood, edged with iron, and spade cultivation in ridged 'lazy-beds' is a technique recognised near Godmanchester and in the Fens. Spades, too, account for the distinctive V-shape of Roman drainage ditches. In recent years villa-fields have been distinguished from 'Celtic' fields of traditional native type. In figs. 21 and 22 two well-known and contrasting cases are shown. At Barnsley Park it is not clear which are paddocks, hoe-plots and ploughed fields. On Brading Down, however, the oblong shape is attributed to the use of a heavier plough (fig. 20, top left) used in one direction and requiring fewer turns at the headland. The coulter cuts the turf and the mouldboard turns a furrow, whose depth is regulated by the share. The more primitive *ard* (on the right) merely grooved the soil but continued to be used through the period on the terraced lynchets and more rectangular plots that still miraculously survive on the southern downs. Such plots were cross-ploughed and often prepared by hoeing.

Although we now know a good deal about some individual estates and regional studies are being energetically pursued, we are not yet able to paint a general picture of the economics of the villa system in Britain. We must accept some major uncertainties, such as the size of the labour force and the relationship between villas and native settlements where much of the labour force lived. Total acreages of estates are much disputed, and the effect of a steadily deteriorating climate has yet to be identified. The balance between resident and absentee landlords, the independence or grouping of villas and the interplay of urban magistracies and landowning gentry in the *civitas* or local government region are all matters that cannot readily be settled from archaeological evidence alone. The orthodox view that villas were clustered around towns and related to major roads is not borne out either by the known distribution or the little we understand of overland routes and rural markets. Scholarly interest is shifting away from the bricks-and-mortar aspects to the social and economic significance of the villas. In this respect particularly the study of Roman Britain has far to go.

7
The end of the villas

The greatest and in many ways the most challenging uncertainty is the fate of the villa system in Britain. One thing, however, is quite clear: the coming of the Saxons was not the cataclysmic event that our sources would have us believe, and the culture of Roman Britain was not extinguished in a sudden blaze of pillage and bloodshed. For by AD 410 — the official end of Roman rule — the 'prior Saxonisation' of Britain had been proceeding for generations through the assimilation of peaceful settlers and the less comfortable presence of officially employed Germanic mercenary garrisons. Moreover, the end of many villas as we know them occurred well before the end of the period — the final phases, for example, of the two villas in figs. 23 and 24 are both dated to the middle of the fourth century. Occupation here continued, though some sites elsewhere were abandoned. But even when we can suggest dates, it is usually impossible to relate the end of a villa to any known event.

At Sparsholt and Gadebridge Park it is paradoxical to find a sub-Roman phase during the Roman period. At Sparsholt the fields continued to be cultivated and the walled yard was maintained as a stockyard, with partial occupation of the derelict aisled building and the creation of a new timbered hall outside the ruins. At Gadebridge Park the baths and villa were demolished and stockades or cattle pens were built over the earlier buildings. Only one small cottage (plate 17) remained in occupation. At Latimer the abandonment of the villa was a gradual, orderly process in the later fourth century; it may be one of the villas that we believe were granted to the Germanic mercenary soldiers (in this case the garrison of neighbouring St Albans), for the succeeding cruck-built hall (plate 16) and adjoining barn are best paralleled in Westphalia. There were four successive sub-Roman building phases lasting well into the dark ages of the fifth century and perhaps beyond. These three sites can now be matched by many others; in each the story is slightly different, but they all have this in common: the new way of life and standards of building leave little archaeological trace, and only recently have our excavation techniques and awareness been able to recover such evidence.

A picture of life in the late fourth century is emerging, at least on a regional scale, from detailed surveys in south-west Britain, Essex and elsewhere. The sub-Roman reoccupation is general, though not universal; we see a move to the security of the refortified towns, with the villas left with bailiffs, granted to immigrant settlers or simply not maintained. A poignant reminder of insecurity in the countryside is the 'corn-drier' that can be seen at Brading, dug through the mosaic floor of the main house (which was apparently rebuilt as an agricultural building).

The evidence for continuity through the dark ages is conflicting and fragmentary, and we have difficulty in even suggesting a time-scale. Either the money economy broke down, or money was just not spent on or in the villas, for we are bereft of our usual aids to close dating, the coins and pottery — a kind of chronological no man's land. The best hypothesis is to suggest that the estates continued to be cultivated as before but free from the pressures of central government, while the domestic buildings were abandoned and even — as the ruins were effectively marginal land — used for cemeteries. Habitations were either dispersed or nucleated around the old sites, forming the beginnings of villages. The continental evidence for this is strong (though a notable lack in Britain is of the fortified, château-like villas). An adaptation of this pattern to Britain would be to suggest the gradual transformation of the villa estate into the medieval manor, especially if, as some believe, feudalism was foreshadowed in the later Empire. So medieval evidence, Saxon estates and parish boundaries are now being examined in the hope of tracing the process backwards in time. One area where the villa estate has been traced in modern landscape is around the Ditchley villa (fig. 25), now largely the estate of its successor, Ditchley Park. Excavation has shown the boundary dykes to be Roman, the gaps between the butt-ends presumably being filled by woodland. Archaeological and documentary evidence suggests that much of the present woodland is ancient, so we can visualise an almost complete circuit of earthwork and forest with a radius of about ¾ mile (1.2 kilometres) around the villa at its centre. The enclosed area of about 875 acres (354 hectares) is bisected by a stream at the bottom of a steep valley and by the approach road to the villa. Within this area can still be seen traces of ancient fields, and at least one subsidiary farm seems to be within the part enclosed by the dykes. The villa itself had a substantial granary, so the other sites shown on fig. 25 may well have been tenant farms outside the estate proper. The country house that succeeded it is less than a mile to the north-west, and the fact that parish boundaries follow much of the presumed Roman boundary suggests that there was here some unit already recognisable in Saxon times.

8
Further reading

General works

Books on villas are not plentiful in any language. The standard work in English is J. Percival: *The Roman Villa: An Historical Introduction* (Batsford, 1976), which has the outstanding merit of treating villas as part of the social and economic life of the Roman world. This Empire-wide view can be supplemented by, for instance, A. G. McKay: *Houses, Villas and Palaces in the Roman World* (Thames & Hudson, 1975), K. D. White: *Roman Farming* (Thames & Hudson, 1970) and chapter 6 of J. Liversidge: *Everyday Life in the Roman Empire* (Batsford, 1976).

For Britain, two essential works are anthologies of varying aspects by several authors. The earlier is A. L. F. Rivet (ed): *The Roman Villa in Britain* (Routledge & Kegan Paul, 1969), complemented by M. Todd (ed): *Studies in the Romano-British Villa* (Leicester University Press, 1978). Most general works on Roman Britain include a chapter on the countryside.

Aspects of villa studies

The difficulty of isolating villas as a self-contained topic is demonstrated by their assimilation into works on many aspects of Romano-British archaeology, such as J. Liversidge: *Britain in the Roman Empire* (Routledge & Kegan Paul, 1968), which is a detailed compendium of information on daily life. The place of villas in the overall picture of rural life was established in A. C. Thomas (ed): *Rural Settlement in Roman Britain* (CBA Research Report no. 7, London 1966) and discussed in copious, if not alway accurate, detail by S. Applebaum in H. P. R. Finberg (ed): *The Agrarian History of England I* (ii) (Cambridge University Press, 1972); see also P. Morris: *Agricultural Buildings in Roman Britain* (British Archaeological Reports no.70, Oxford 1979). For the relationship with the towns, the standard work is A. L. F. Rivet: *Town and Country in Roman Britain* (Hutchinson, 1958); a slighter and more localised essay on the same theme is K. Branigan: *Town and Country: Verulamium and the Roman Chilterns* (Spurbooks, 1973).

Regional studies

An important regional survey is K. Branigan: *The Roman Villa in South-west England* (Moonraker Press, 1977); this is now joined by E. W. Black: *The Roman Villas of South-east England* (British Archaeological Reports no.171, Oxford, 1987). Individual counties were covered long ago by the series of the *Victoria County Histories* and more recently by the volumes of the Royal Commission on Historical Monuments; by county surveys such as A. D. McWhirr: *Roman Gloucestershire* (Alan Sutton, Gloucester, 1981) and the chapters on Essex, Hertfordshire, Northamptonshire, Hampshire and the Isle of Wight in the volume (above) edited by M. Todd.

Individual sites

Detailed references to British villas would double the size of this book and can be found in the bibliographies of the general works mentioned above. But beware: some sites are published in generous detail as books, while others are merely frustrating and inadequate summaries. Several excavations, inevitably, still await publication. The locations of all known villas are given on the Ordnance Survey's *Map of Roman Britain* (fourth edition, 1980) and details of how to find the principal ones will be found in the many archaeological guides and gazetteers, notably R. J. A. Wilson: *A Guide to the Roman Remains in Britain* (Constable, third edition 1988). See also D. E. Johnston (ed): *Discovering Roman Britain* (Shire Publications, second edition 1993).

Note: in the following plans H indicates a hypocaust, M a mosaic, and T a tessellated floor.

Fig. 1. *(Opposite top)* Newton St Loe, Avon. Two adjacent family houses.
Fig. 2. *(Opposite bottom)* Rockbourne, Hampshire. The skeleton found in the hypocaust room was evidently someone killed while robbing the masonry, while the other was a burial, presumably post-Roman.

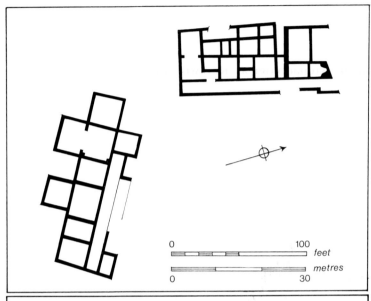

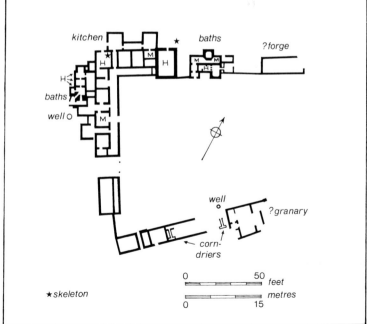

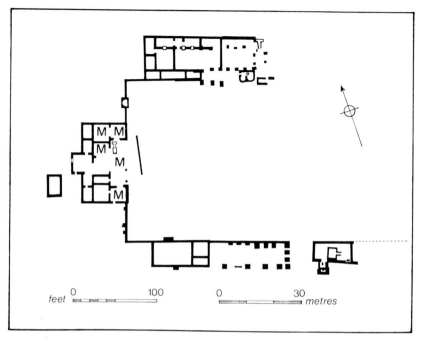

Fig. 3. Brading, Isle of Wight, as excavated. In its latest phase the main house has been gutted and partly rerofed, forming an open-fronted work-hall and stores. A 'corn-drier' has been inserted through the mosaic floor.

Fig. 4. *(Opposite)* Bignor, West Sussex. Intermediate and final plans, with suggested 'accommodation units' in successive versions of the north wing. (After E. W. Black and F. G. Aldsworth.)

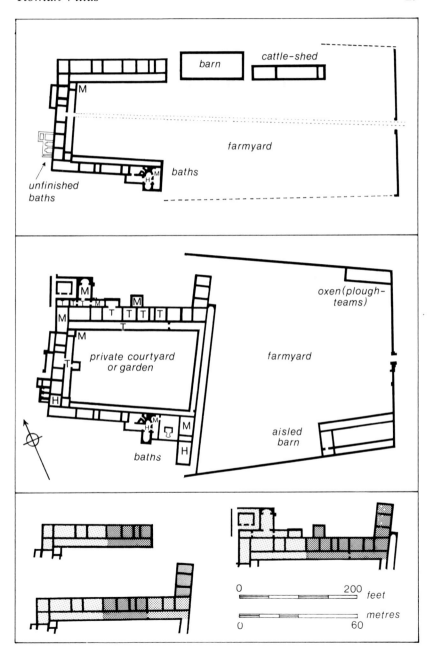

barn

cattle-shed

M

farmyard

baths

M
H

unfinished
baths

oxen (plough-
teams)

M

T T M

M

M

T T T T

T

M

private courtyard
or garden

farmyard

T

H

M
H

M

baths

H

aisled
barn

0   200
feet

metres
0   60

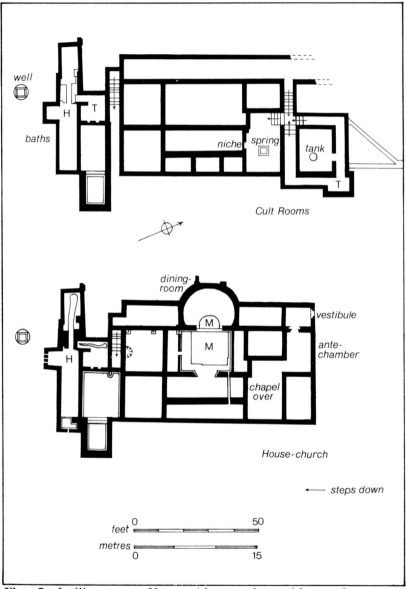

Fig. 5. Lullingstone, Kent. Above: the evidence for pagan worship in the second century. Below: fourth-century modifications including the house-church.

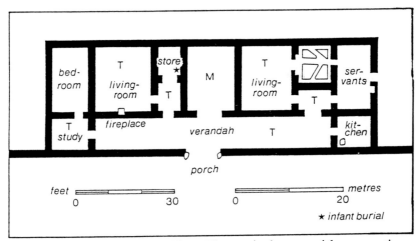

Fig. 6. Sparsholt, Hampshire. The main house with suggestions for the use of rooms. The infant burial may be a dedication.

Fig. 7. Lockleys, Hertfordshire. The villa as it may have looked in the fourth century AD (after H. C. Lander).

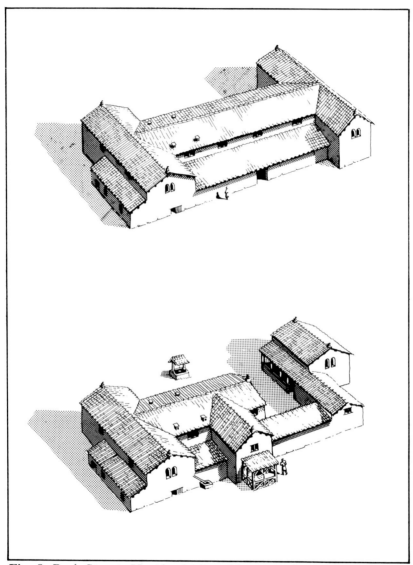

Fig. 8. Park Street, Hertfordshire. Above: as it may have looked in the late second century AD. Below: its final fourth-century state (after N. Davey).

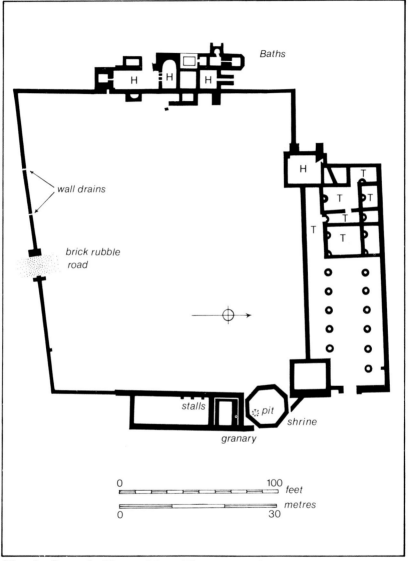

Fig. 9. Stroud, Hampshire. The unusually large bath suite and possible shrine suggest that this was the focus of a large estate. The stalls were probably for three plough teams of oxen, and the wall-drains imply either an unrecognised timber lean-to shed or a dung heap.

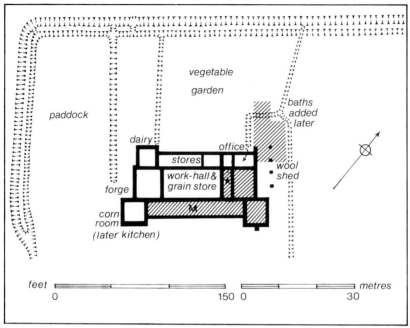

Fig. 10. Frocester Court, Gloucestershire, in the early fourth century AD, with suggested use of rooms. Residential quarters on the ground floor are shaded, and stairs are asterisked.

Fig. 11. Chedworth, Gloucestershire. A new reconstruction (after S. Gibson).

Fig. 12. Latimer, Buckinghamshire. A reconstruction, showing the gardens as they might have looked (after K. Branigan).

Fig. 13. Frocester Court, Gloucestershire. Excavated evidence for the garden.

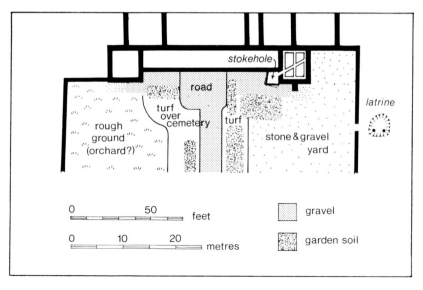

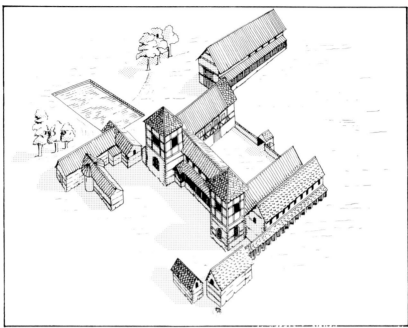

Fig. 14. Gadebridge Park, Hertfordshire (after D. S. Neal). The
tower-like granaries used the warmth of hypocausts below. Note
the swimming pool.

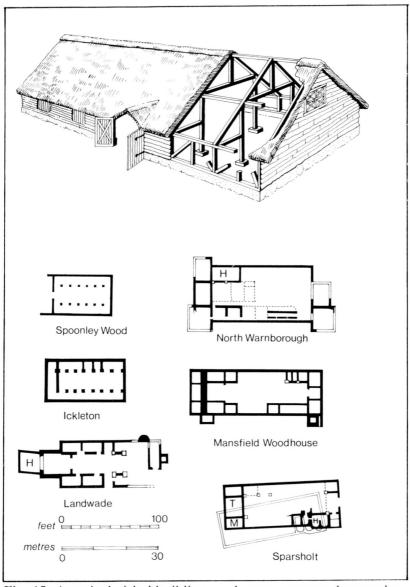

Fig. 15. A typical aisled building, and some excavated examples.

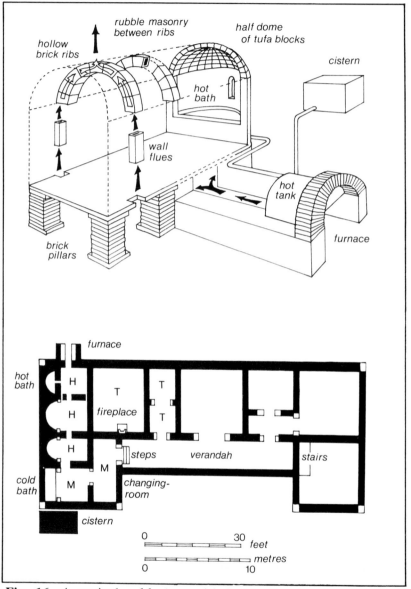

Fig. 16. A typical *caldarium* with hot bath, showing details of plumbing and insulation. The box-flues often covered the entire wall. Below: the main house at Newport, Isle of Wight.

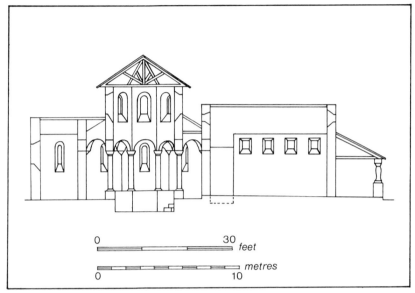

Fig. 17. Lufton, Somerset. A conjectural elevation of the baths (after L. C. Hayward).

Fig. 18. Left: a villa sketched on the wall plaster at Hucclecote, Gloucestershire (drawing by R. G. Collingwood). Right: a tiny model ploughman from Piercebridge, Co. Durham (drawn by M. O. Miller). (Both reproduced by courtesy of the Trustees of the British Museum.)

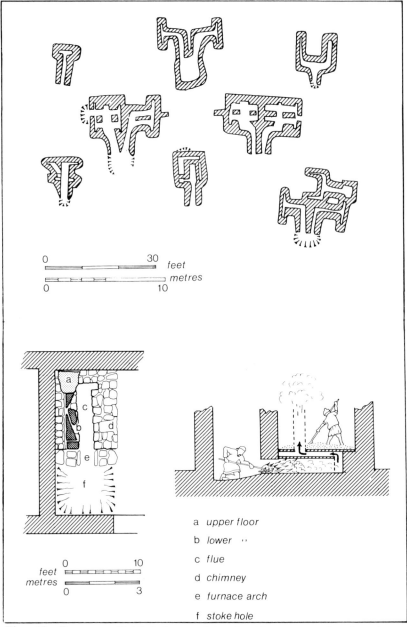

0 feet
0 metres 10
30 feet

feet 0 10
metres 0 3

a upper floor
b lower „
c flue
d chimney
e furnace arch
f stoke hole

Fig. 19. Romano-British 'corn-driers'. Above: a selection from the series at the Hambleden villa, Buckinghamshire. Below: Atworth, Wiltshire.

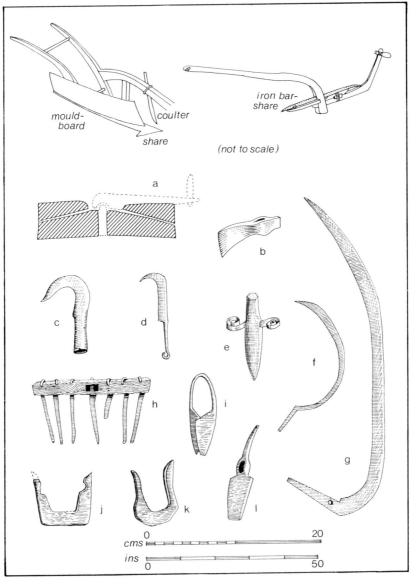

Fig. 20. Above: a plough of Roman type and a typical iron age ard. Below: farm implements from British sites: *a*, oscillatory quern; *b*, axe; *c*, billhook; *d*, pruning hook; *e*, mower's anvil; *f*, sickle; *g*, scythe; *h*, wooden hay-rake; *i*, sheep shears; *j*, *k*, iron bindings for wooden spades; *l*, mattock or hoe. The wooden handles are missing.

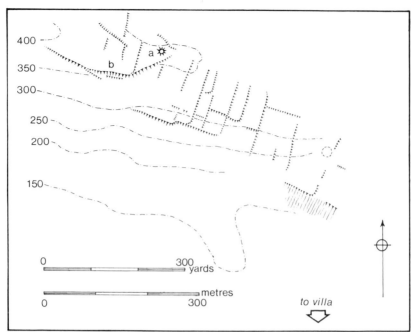

Fig. 21. Fields associated with the Brading villa, Isle of Wight. At *a,* a bronze age barrow has been incorporated, and at *b* there are traces of a flattened pre-Roman earthwork, perhaps a hillfort. Contours in feet.

Fig. 22. Emparkment at Barnsley Park, Gloucestershire, has preserved the faint earthworks of Roman fields and enclosures. Those immediately to the north, west and south of the villa are stonewalled, perhaps stockyards. Selective excavation has suggested a complex history extending into the fifth century AD. Contours in feet.

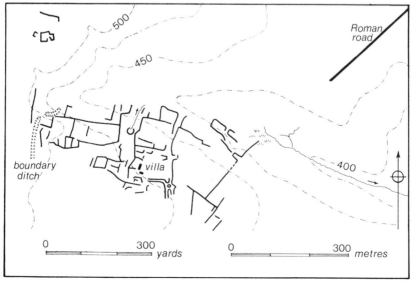

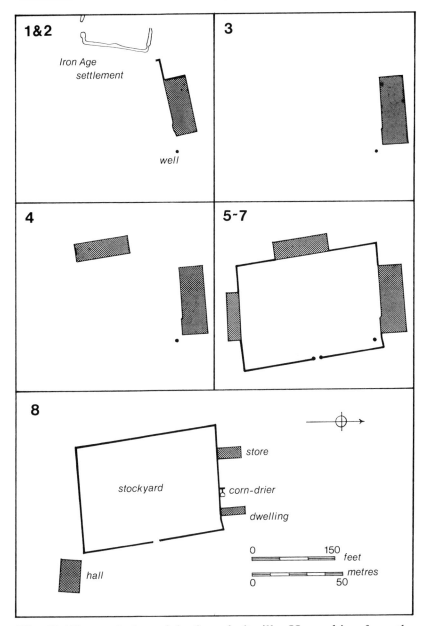

Fig. 23. The evolution of the Sparsholt villa, Hampshire, from the second to the fourth centuries AD. In the final phase the courtyard was kept as a stockyard, the derelict buildings were used as stores or demolished, and a new timber-framed hall was built outside the south-east corner.

44   *Roman Villas*

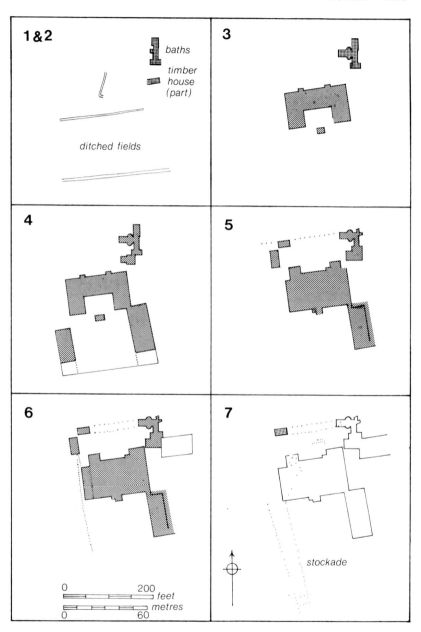

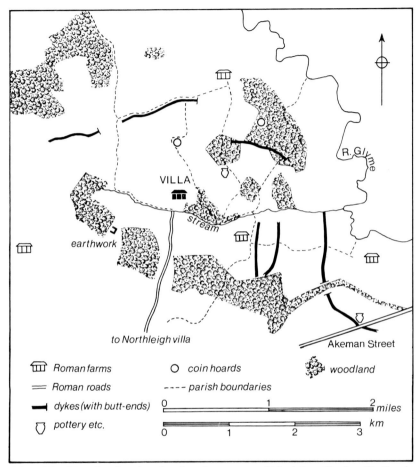

Fig. 25. Continuity in the landscape at Ditchley Park, Oxfordshire. The main villa is shown on plate 6.

Fig. 24. *(Opposite)* The evolution of the Gadebridge Park villa, Hertfordshire, from the late first to the fourth centuries AD. In the final phase the baths and villa were demolished and stockades or cattle pens were built on their sites. The two-roomed cottage is shown on plate 17. Occupation may have extended into the fifth century AD.

Plate 1. Portrait of the owner or his wife? A wall painting from the baths at Sparsholt, Hampshire. Found in fragments, it has been reconstructed by Dr N. Davey. (Crown copyright.)

Plate 2. Great Witcombe, Gloucestershire. This delectable setting proved treacherous, as the hillside is riddled with springs and soil-slip required constant buttressing and rebuilding of the villa. The water was used ornamentally, and the octagonal shrine in the foreground was probably dedicated to water deities. (Author.)

Plate 3. Cropmarks of a small unexcavated house on the site of a large iron age settlement at Bazely Copse, Micheldever, Hampshire. (University of Cambridge: copyright reserved.)

Plate 4. Cropmarks of unexcavated rectangular and circular houses, south-east of Great Doddington, Northamptonshire (University of Cambridge: copyright reserved.)

Plate 5. Sparsholt, Hampshire, under excavation. The main house has been excavated and backfilled; it overlies the ditches of earlier Roman field boundaries and an even earlier iron age ditched settlement, with circular storage pits. (P. Walters.)

Plate 6. Cropmarks of the walled villa and field boundaries at Ditchley, Oxfordshire. (Ashmolean Museum.)

Plate 7. The grandeur of a big villa is suggested by this reconstruction of the main house at Littlecote. (Painting by L. Thompson, copyright Roman Research Trust, Littlecote.)

Plate 8. Newport, Isle of Wight, as it may have appeared in the third century AD. (Drawing by D. Tomalin.)

Plate 9. Rapsley, Ewhurst, Surrey, as it may have appeared about AD 280-330. (Drawing by C. de la Nougerede.)

Plate 10. Cropmarks of an unexcavated villa at Radwell, Hertfordshire. The principal house is thought to lie beside the river at the top of the photograph. (University of Cambridge: copyright reserved.)

Plate 11. Sparsholt, Hampshire. The superimposed aisled buildings under excavation. The baths of both can be seen at the bottom left. (P. Walters.)

Plate 12. A pottery sherd inscribed with Greek letters from Chalk, Kent. (Southampton University.)

Plate 13. Stone roof finials from Dewlish, Dorset (left) and Rockbourne, Hampshire (right). (Dorset Institute of Higher Education and M. J. Locke.)

Plate 14. A drain in the villa at Darenth, Kent. It flushed the latrines in the baths (off the picture, right), ran below the room in the foreground and discharged into the river. (An unpublished photograph of *c.* 1895.)

Plate 15. The baths at Dicket Mead under excavation. The cold room and plunge bath are in the foreground; the hypocaust of the hot room is visible, with the hot bath to the left. Beyond the arch stood the hot tank and the furnace room is in the distance. (J. Dettmar.)

Plate 16. *(Opposite top)* The fourth-century post-villa building at Latimer, Buckinghamshire, as excavated. Its cruck-built construction is shown by the settings for upright timbers just inside the walls. (K. Branigan.)

Plate 17. *(Opposite bottom)* The two-roomed cottage of the fifth century at Gadebridge Park, Hertfordshire, as excavated. The kitchen, with ovens, hearth and storage cist, is the further room. (J. Brown.)

Plate 18. Lullingstone, Kent, as it may have appeared *c.* AD 360. The small circular temple was demolished shortly after the construction of the temple-mausoleum to the left. The end of the large barn can be seen bottom left. (Drawing by A. Sorrell; Crown copyright reserved.)

Plate 19. A typical Roman roof of limestone slates at Kingscote, Gloucestershire. Reconstruction using original materials. (Author.)

Plate 20. A reconstruction of a Romano-British interior as it might have looked *c.* AD 100. (Copyright: Museum of London.)

Plate 21. A typical Romano-British kitchen reconstructed. (Copyright: Museum of London.)

Plate 22. A corn mill on an Italian villa; fragments of these mills are occasionally found in Britain. (Author.)

Plate 23. Winnowing: from a bas-relief. (Author.)

Villas to visit

Few of the villas listed below are visible in anything like their entirety. Unfortunately, there are none in the north of England yet. Grid references are shown in brackets, and some guidance is given to when the sites are open; opening times, however, are liable to change, and intending visitors are advised to check before making a special journey.

Bancroft, Milton Keynes (SP 8340). The excavations were completed in 1986. The villa is in part of the city parks network and access is not restricted. Park off Millers Way. The villa is now marked out on site, with the fishpool reconstructed and information panels. Telephone: 0908 312475.

Bignor, West Sussex (SU 9814). The main residential quarters are attractively set out, with earlier phases indicated in coloured concrete. Mosaics and site museum are displayed *in situ*, in grouped buildings that resemble a straggling villa. Open regularly in summer. Telephone: 07987 259.

Brading, Isle of Wight (SZ 6086). Most of the main west wing, with its mystical mosaics, and the well of the north wing are displayed under modern buildings. Open daily April to September and winter by arrangement. Telephone: 0983 406223 (summer) and 529963 (winter).

Carisbrooke, Isle of Wight (SZ 4888). The villa (with one mosaic) was excavated in 1859 and has since deteriorated. At the time of writing (1993) it is still on private land and not open to the public. It has, however, been acquired by the Isle of Wight County Council, and it is planned to open it, with an explanatory display, in the mid 1990s.

Chedworth, Gloucestershire (SP 0513). The complete villa is displayed in an attractive rural setting, with the main house (with mosaics) and baths under cover. There is a museum and visitors' centre. Open regularly from February to December. Telephone: 0242 890256.

Dicket Mead, Welwyn (Welwyn Roman Baths), Hertfordshire (TL 2315). A villa bath-house enterprisingly preserved under the A1 motorway. Open Sunday afternoons and bank holidays, other times by appointment. Telephone: 0707 271362.

Great Witcombe, Gloucestershire (SO 8914). This well-preserved and attractively sited villa has been reopened after conservation. A fine bath-house at the south-west corner has mosaics *in situ*. The key is available at the farm.

Keynsham, Avon (ST 6569). Fragments of the north wing only are visible near the mortuary chapel. The mosaics are in store and inaccessible (1993).

Kings Weston, Avon (ST 5377). The baths and most of the residential rooms of this winged corridor villa are visible, with two mosaics (one from nearby Brislington). The key is available from Blaise Castle House Museum, Henbury, Bristol. Telephone: 0272 506789 for enquiries. A guide-book is available from Blaise Castle House Museum or from Bristol City Museum and Art Gallery.

Littlecote Park, Hungerford, Berkshire (SU 2970). Excavation of this complex courtyard villa is now complete, the Orpheus mosaic conserved and the walls marked out on site. It was open to the public in 1993, but its future is uncertain; for information on whether and when it will be open in subsequent years, telephone 0488 684000.

Lullingstone, Kent (TQ 5365). Most of this fine house, with mosaics and cult rooms, is displayed under a modern building in an attractive riverside setting. The temple-mausoleum is not officially accessible. Open regularly in summer. Telephone: 0322 863467.

Newport, Isle of Wight (SZ 5088). Entered now from Cypress Road, this winged corridor villa with fine bath-suite is preserved under a modern cover building with an exhibition room and a Roman garden. Open from Easter to the end of September daily except Saturdays; in winter by appointment. Telephone: 0983 529720 (summer) and 529963 (winter).

North Leigh, Oxfordshire (SP 3915). Signposted from the road and reached on foot by a lane, two wings of this large courtyard villa are displayed and are accessible at all times. The conserved triclinium mosaic is under a cover building which is occasionally opened to the public (see noticeboard on site); it can be viewed at all times through a window.

Orpington, Bromley, London (TQ 4566). Known locally as the Crofton Roman Villa and excavated in 1988, the surviving ten rooms of this modest but well preserved villa house were conserved under a cover building and opened to the public in 1993. Five rooms have hypocausts (both pillared and channelled), but no mosaics. It is in Crofton Road, next to Orpington railway station and the the Civic Halls, and car parking is usually possible nearby. Open Mondays, Wednesdays, Fridays and Sunday afternoons from April to October or by appointment. Telephone 081-462 4737 or 0689 873826.

Orton Longueville, Cambridgeshire (TL 1598). The main villa buildings have not been excavated, but an aisled building, a well and a possible temple are marked out in the recreation ground, with part of a military ditch.

Rockbourne, Hampshire (SU 1217). This extensive courtyard villa is marked out and conserved, including a unique hypocaust, a 'corn-drier' and two mosaics. There is a site museum. Open regularly in summer and at other times by appointment. Telephone: 0962 846304.

Other sites

The so-called 'villa' at Colliton Park, Dorchester, is strictly a town-house of Roman Dorchester. It lies behind the County Hall, is well displayed with one mosaic and is worth a visit at any time. Some excavated sites, on the other hand, are so overgrown that the visitor may have difficulty in finding even the walls; these include Titsey, Surrey (TQ 4054), Wadfield, Gloucestershire (SP 0226) with its neighbour Spoonley Wood (SP 0425), and Worsham Bottom, Oxfordshire (SP 3011), at all of which permission should be sought locally. The outline of the Sparsholt villa, Hampshire (ST 4130) is to be indicated with explanatory signs, but no masonry will be exposed; a full size replica of part is planned at the Butser Archaeological Farm, Hampshire (SU 717166). The remains of Llantwit Major (SS 9569) and Cae Summerhouse (SS 8677), two of the few villas in Wales, are now merely faint earthworks in meadows.

Index

Numbers in italic refer to pages with illustrations.